LEADER

FATHOM BIBLE STUDIES

FATHM

A DEEP DIVE INTO THE STORY OF GOD

the bible

WHERE IT CAME FROM AND HOW TO READ IT

FATHOM: THE BIBLE
WHERE IT CAME FROM AND HOW TO READ IT
LEADER GUIDE

Writer: Bart Patton
Editor: Ben Howard
Designer: Keely Moore

Websites are constantly changing. Although the websites recommended in this resource were checked at the time this unit was developed, we recommend that you double-check all sites to verify that they are still live and that they are still suitable for students before doing the activity.

ISBN: 9781501837739

PACP10508410-01

17 18 19 20 21 22 23 24 25 26 — 10 9 8 7 6 5 4 3 2 1

MANUFACTURED IN THE UNITED STATES OF AMERICA

CONTENTS

About Fathom

Fathom.

It's such a big word. It feels endless and deep. It's the kind of word that feels like it should only be uttered by James Earl Jones with the bass turned all the way up.

Which means it's the perfect word to talk about a God who's infinite and awe-inspiring. It's also the perfect word for a book like the Bible that's filled with miracles and inspiration, but also wrestles with stories of violence and pain and loss.

The mission of *Fathom* is to dive deep into the story of God that we find in the Bible. You'll encounter Scriptures filled with inspiration and encouragement, and you'll also explore passages that are more complicated and challenging.

Each lesson will focus on one passage, but will also launch into the larger context of how God's story is being told through that passage. More importantly, each lesson will explore how God's story is intimately tied to our own stories, and how a God who is beyond our imagination can also be a God who loves us deeply and personally.

We invite you to wrestle with this and more as we dive deep into God's story.

How to Use This Book

First, we want to thank you for teaching this class! While we strive to provide the best material possible for leaders and students, we know that your personal connection with your teens is the most important part of the lesson.

With that out of the way, welcome to the *Fathom Leader Guide*. Each lesson is designed around Kolb's Learning Cycle and moves students through five sections: *Sync, Tour, Reveal, Build,* and *After.*

Sync introduces the students to the general theme of each lesson with a fun activity. There is both a high-energy and low-energy option to choose from in each lesson. *Tour* is the meat of the lesson and focuses intensely on the central Scripture each week. *Reveal* is a time for reflection where youth can digest the information they've heard and start to make to process it. Then the *Build* section puts this newfound knowledge to practice using creative activities and projects. Finally, *After* gives the students options for practices to try throughout the week to reinforce the central concept of the lesson.

Additionally, before each lesson, a Theology and Commentary section is provided to give you a little more information about the topic being discussed that week.

This Leader Guide is designed to be used hand-in-hand with the *Fathom Student Journal.* Each student will need a journal, and the journals should be kept in the class at the end of the lesson. At the end of the study, give the students their journals as a keepsake to remember what they've learned.

Finally, at the end of this book we've included an Explore More section that offers short outlines for additional lessons if you and your class want to keep diving into these Scriptures after the end of this four-week study.

The Fathom 66

ENTER ZIP OR LOCATION [   ]

Stories ♡

★★★★★

TICKETS

Showtimes: Parts of Genesis, Joshua, Judges, Ruth, 1 Samuel,
2 Samuel, 1 Kings, 2 Kings, 1 Chronicles, 2 Chronicles, Ezra,
Nehemiah, Esther, Matthew, Mark, Luke, John, Acts

The Law ♡

★★★★★

TICKETS

Showtimes: Parts of Genesis, Exodus, Leviticus, Numbers,
Deuteronomy

Wisdom ♡

★★★★★

TICKETS

Showtimes: Job, Some Psalms, Proverbs, Ecclesiastes,
Song of Solomon, Lamentations, James

Psalms ♡

★★★★★

TICKETS

Showtimes: Psalms

The Prophets ♡

★★★★★

TICKETS

Showtimes: Isaiah, Jeremiah, Ezekiel, Hosea, Joel, Amos, Obadiah,
Jonah, Micah, Nahum, Habakkuk, Zephaniah, Haggai, Zechariah,
Malachi

Letters ♡

★★★★★

TICKETS

Showtimes: Romans, 1 Corinthians, 2 Corinthians, Galatians, Ephesians,
Philippians, Colossians, 1 Thessalonians, 2 Thessalonians, 1 Timothy, 2 Timothy,
Titus, Philemon, Hebrews, James, 1 Peter, 2 Peter, 1 John, 2 John, 3 John, Jude

Apocalyptic Writings ♡

★★★★★

TICKETS

Showtimes: Daniel, Revelation

The Fathom Bible Storylines

Create **1**

Invite **I**

Act **A**

Redeem **R**

Experience **E**

Hope **H**

Introduction to The Bible

Background

The Bible we study today is a collection of 66 books—39 in the Old Testament and 27 in the New Testament—comprised of laws, histories, stories, poems, and letters exploring God's relationship with humanity. These books were originally written in three languages: Hebrew in the Old Testament, Greek in the New Testament, and Aramaic in the Books of Ezra and Daniel, as well as various other passages. Today the Bible is the most translated book of all time and is available in over five hundred different languages.

It only makes sense that a book written and compiled over hundreds of years by dozens of writers would be complicated and sometimes confusing. Add to that language differences and the need to wade through a variety of genres, and the Bible can look downright daunting.

This study is about empowering your students to begin that task. Over the next four lessons, they'll learn about the history of the Bible and the types of stories it tells. More importantly, they'll learn and practice the methods they'll need to read and understand the Bible for themselves.

In some ways, the Bible is like a treasure chest. It's filled to the brim with riches, if only you can find the key to unlock it. It's a book filled with stories of courage and wisdom, inspiration and practical advice; but above all, it's a book that gives us insight into a God who is both far bigger than we can ever imagine and by our side at all times. This study, if they're willing, will help your students find the key to unlocking this holy book and all that it has to offer.

Fathom Strategy for Reading and Understanding the Bible

"The Bible is written for us, but not to us."

This where we start on our quest. When we read the Bible, we have to constantly remember that the Bible is written for us, but not to us. Understanding the original context of the Bible helps us ask the right questions when interpreting Scripture.

For the first steps in our process, we need to understand how each passage we read functions in context and examine the historical background. When we read a passage, we should ask questions about the era, location, and culture of the original audience, as well as how a particular writing relates to the larger narrative of the Bible. This strategy not only helps us understand a passage's primary meaning, it also gives us guidance on how to translate that meaning into our specific circumstances today.

Working Definitions

Canon—the books of the Bible collectively recognized by the Christian church throughout time as inspired by God

Covenant—a solemn promise between God and God's people that defines their relationship to one another

Exegesis—the critical process of explaining and interpreting the Bible

Inductive Bible Study—a type of study that moves from generalized thoughts to specific application by using the Bible as the primary source of understanding

Lectio Divina (Divine Reading)—an ancient Latin practice of reading Scripture that involves reading, meditation, and prayer

FATH●M
A History of the Bible

Summary

Students will gain an understanding of how we have come to have the Bible we read and use today.

Overview

- **Sync** with the concepts of transmission and translation through a group activity.
- **Tour** through the history of the Bible, introducing the key concepts of inspiration, transmission, and translation.
- **Reveal** how inspiration, transmission, and translation can affect our faith through journaling.
- **Build** understanding of the Christian tradition of translation through an activity that allows students to personalize the history they have learned.
- **After** the lesson, apply these ideas through activities that encourage the use of multiple translations of the Bible.

Anchor Point

- 2 Timothy 3:16-17—*Every scripture is inspired by God and is useful for teaching, for showing mistakes, for correcting, and for training character, so that the person who belongs to God can be equipped to do everything that is good.*

Supplies

- Student Journals
- Pens or pencils
- Ream of blank paper
- Stapler

Parent E-mail

We are beginning our new study on how to read and understand the Bible with a lesson that will help youth learn about how we came to have the Bible we read today. They will learn about important concepts like inspiration, transmission, and translation. Here are some ways to engage this week:

- Show them family Bibles that have been passed down.
- If your child does not have a Bible of her or his own, allow the youth to pick one out online or at a bookstore.
- Ask the youth to explain the lesson to you.

Leader Notes

"How did we get the Bible?" "Who wrote it?" "How do we know that the Bible is true?" When left unanswered, these questions are the first roadblocks young people face when engaging Scripture. The origins of the Bible are powerful, and understanding them helps us gain confidence in our grasp of even the most difficult passages. This lesson will help students understand how we came to have the Bible as we know it, guide youth through a history of the Bible, and introduce the key concepts of inspiration, transmission, and translation.

Theology and Commentary

Inspiration

The popular expression of the doctrine of biblical inspiration is largely based on 2 Timothy 3:16. The word translated in English as "inspired" is *theopneustos* in the original Greek—literally meaning "divinely breathed into."

There are many theories explaining the process of inspiration. Dictation Theories propose that God spoke the exact words in the original documents and humans wrote them down, so every word in the Bible is the very Word of God. The Neo-Orthodox Theory argues that the Bible is primarily the human account of God's larger revelation. In this theory, Jesus is the Word of God—or ultimate revelation of God—and the Scriptures bear witness to Christ. Limited Inspiration Theories present the Bible as primarily human writings with very little divine guidance.

It's important to understand biblical inspiration as a divine mystery. While the doctrine of inspiration helps us affirm that God is the ultimate "author" of the Bible, we should strive to seek balance in our practical understanding of inspiration. When we regard the Bible as too sacred, it becomes cold and distant—a book to be feared. When we view it as merely human, it begins to lose its authority. A Wesleyan understanding of inspiration is one that leaves room for balance and conversation. Wesleyan tradition holds that human authors divinely inspired by the Holy Spirit indeed wrote the Bible, but also proposes that these human authors were given great freedom in their expression of God's revelation (not dictation). The Bible is certainly authoritative as Divine Revelation, but it is to be understood through the distinctly human nature of its writing. For Wesleyans, the Bible reveals the Word of God given to humanity.

Transmission

Transmission is the process through which the original stories and writings of the Bible were dispersed. Before the printing press, hand-copied manuscripts were the only way to copy and distribute important writings. While there are no known original "source" documents of biblical writings, we have over 5,500 manuscripts of the New Testament alone transmitted from the ancient world. The sheer volume of New Testament manuscripts is overwhelming when compared to other well-known ancient documents without original "source" documents—like the writings of Plato, Aristotle, and the historian Pliny—that are considered authentic today. There is no doubt that God was at work in the transmission of the Scriptures just as God was at work in its inspiration. These manuscripts help us to understand the history of how the Bible came together, as well as bolstering our confidence in its reliability.

Translation

Translation is the process of rendering a text from one language into another language. Since the Bible was originally written and transmitted in Hebrew, Greek, and Aramaic, we largely rely on translations in our churches today. Because of the vast differences between these ancient languages and modern English, there are a variety of theories about how best to translate the Bible. Some translations emphasize a more literal, word-for-word formal method. This is known as Verbal Equivalence. Translators using this method search for the best word-for-word match from the original language while taking into context order and syntax. Other translations employ a more pragmatic, or thought-for-thought method. Much like our own writing and speech, Scripture is full of idioms that don't hold their meanings well when translated word-for-word. Translators using this approach seek to recast the larger ideas of the original words into our language. This is called Dynamic Equivalence. A paraphrased translation is an extreme version of the Dynamic Equivalence method that adds words to the original text in an effort to clearly convey the original meaning.

Leader Reflection

I met John a few years ago. When he discovered I was a youth minister, he said, "I *really* need to talk to you! You see, my wife and I are interested in starting some kind of religion, but we don't know which one. A few weeks ago, I invited a priest, a rabbi, an Imam, a Jehovah's Witness, a Christian pastor, and a Buddhist monk over to my house for dinner. We had a wonderful dinner and then I asked them to tell me what they were all about."

I was astounded. "So what did you think?"

"Well, I don't know. We were both impressed with the Christian pastor and what he believes about the Bible. He actually believes in the Bible—that it's from God and that it helps him. I've got tons of respect for that. The others seemed afraid of the Bible, or made me afraid of it, or didn't care about it at all."

"So what's the problem?" I pushed.

"Well, my wife knows the pastor because she works near his church. And, well, he's a jerk. I don't understand believing something so amazing if it's not changing who you are."

It's one thing to have a high opinion of the Bible. It's another thing entirely to allow the Scriptures to change us in tangible ways. We need a working relationship with the Bible. As you prepare to teach, pray that God will drive fear, apathy, and rigidity away from our hearts when it comes to the Bible.

NOTES

SYNC (10-15 minutes)

High-Energy Option—So You Think You Can Dance

SAY: I'm going to break you into three groups. I'll need one volunteer dance teacher from each group. We're going to go into a separate space where the rest can't see us, and I'm going to teach you a dance. Each of you will write down instructions for the dance in your own words. You will then come back and teach the dance to your group. Once you've taught your group the dance, we will have a dance-off.

[Show the three volunteers the simple six-step dance move below. Perform the dance at least three times. Do not explain the dance or give instructions. Give them a few minutes to write down instructions for the dance. Bring the dance teachers back to their groups.]

The Dance Move
1. Left leg step out, left arm folded on hip.
2. Hands joined, arms make a circle from left to right across the body.
3. Clap.
4. Right leg front kick.
5. Take three steps back starting with the left leg.
6. Stretch right hand high in the air.

SAY: Without performing the dance, each teacher is going to teach his or her group the dance only from spoken descriptions. Teachers may not demonstrate the dance. I'll give you a few minutes to learn. Each group will then perform their dance for the whole group. I need a group to volunteer to go first, second, and third.

[Give each group five minutes to learn the dance. Then allow each group to perform their dance as a team. You may give scores and choose a winning group.]

ASK:
1. How were the group's dances different?
2. Were there things about the dance that all groups did the same?

SAY: This activity involved three processes: inspiration, transmission, and translation. The three dance teachers were inspired when they saw the original dance. Their writings transmitted the instructions of the dance. Then, each group translated their teacher's writings into a dance. Today we will examine these processes in the history of the Bible.

Low-Energy Option—Cool Story, Bro

[Make stacks of nine pieces of paper for every student. Staple each stack in a top corner before the game.]

SAY: Everyone sit in a circle. I'm giving each of you a stack of paper and a pen or pencil. Write a sentence on the first sheet of paper. Do not share your sentence with anyone. Make it random, and make sure it has a noun and a verb! Now pass your papers to the left. Illustrate your neighbor's sentence with drawings only—no numbers, letters, or symbols—on the next blank piece of paper.

[Give them one minute to draw.]

SAY: Fold the first sheet back so that your drawing is on top of the stack. Pass your paper stacks to the left. Now, write a sentence describing your neighbor's drawing on the next blank piece of paper without looking at the first sentence.

[Repeat the drawing/sentence pattern until the paper stacks are full. Be sure to end with a sentence.]

SAY: Without flipping through the papers, try to find your original paper stack based on the final sentence written.

ASK:
1. Was the final sentence on your paper anywhere close to your original sentence?
2. Even if sentences changed dramatically, were there subjects, verbs, or themes that still made it through?

SAY: This activity involved three processes: inspiration, transmission, and translation. The first sentence inspired the first drawing. The message of the sentence was transmitted and translated through writings and drawings around the circle. Today we will examine these processes in the history of the Bible.

TOUR (15-20 minutes)

ASK: How do you think we got the Bible?

[Affirm every response. After giving everyone an opportunity to answer, ask a second question.]

ASK: Does it matter how we got the Bible? Why or why not?

[Affirm all responses to allow for a good discussion. After several minutes . . .]

SAY: There seems to be a lot of confusion around the Bible and how we use it. Understanding the history of the Bible gives us confidence that the Bible is a reliable source of God's revelation throughout human history and for our lives today. Our understanding of the Bible's history also helps us understand better how to read it. I need a volunteer to read 2 Timothy 3:16-17.

[Volunteer reads 2 Timothy 3:16-17.]

- 2 Timothy 3:16-17—*Every scripture is inspired by God and is useful for teaching, for showing mistakes, for correcting, and for training character, so that the person who belongs to God can be equipped to do everything that is good.*

SAY: The apostle Paul, in his second letter to his young disciple Timothy, presents ideas about the significance of the Bible in our everyday lives. What does this verse say about the Scriptures?

[Help the students affirm the concepts of "inspired," "useful for teaching, for showing mistakes, for correcting, and for training character," and "equipped."]

SAY: Our earlier activity helped us understand just a little bit about the inspiration, transmission, and translation of information. These three key concepts help us understand how we have the Bible we do today.

[Introduce these concepts and help the students understand them. Have them write down in their journals the basic definition for each concept.]

Inspiration—the process by which the Holy Spirit initiates communication from God.

Transmission—the process by which the original stories and writings of the Bible were dispersed, including by manuscripts and oral tradition. The core message is broadcast beyond the original sources.

Translation—the process of reproducing the meaning of something that exists in one language in another language.

[Walk the students through the provided History of the Bible Timeline. Ask the students to consider the order of events as they relate to the writing, transmission, and translation of the Bible.]

ASK: Which of these events or time periods are you already familiar with? Where do you see the three processes at work in this timeline?

History of the Bible Timeline

Pre-History	Oral traditions and storytelling (Insp)
3200 BC	Early Mesopotamian/Sumerian writings
2000 BC	Birth of Abraham
2000–1500 BC	Book of Job written (possibly) (Insp)
1500 BC	Moses receives the Law on Mount Sinai (Insp)
1000 BC	Israel begins recording history; David is king (Insp) (Transm)
621 BC	Book of the Law discovered in temple by King Josiah (2 Kings 22) (Transm)
587 BC	Jerusalem destroyed; ancient Israelite writings compiled in captivity (Transm)
250–135 BC	Books of our Old Testament translated into Greek Septuagint (Transl)
200 BC–AD 70	Dead Sea Scrolls written in Essene community (Old Testament) (Transm)
AD 30	Ministry of Jesus
AD 52	Paul writes first letter to Thessalonian church (Insp)
AD 70	Mark writes his Gospel (Insp)
AD 80–90	Luke writes his Gospel and the Acts of the Apostles (Insp)
AD 80–100	Matthew writes his Gospel (Insp)

AD 100	Last of the New Testament books written
AD 350	Books and segments of the Bible translated into Latin (Transl)
AD 383–405	Jerome's Latin Vulgate (Transl)
AD 393	Council of Hippo defines New Testament books
AD 397	Council of Carthage issues a complete canon of the Bible
AD 600–1100	Masoretic Text of Hebrew Scriptures compiled (Transm)
AD 1225	Present system of chapters added
AD 1382	Bible translated into Middle English by John Wycliffe (Transl)
AD 1455	Gutenberg makes first printed Bible with movable type (in Latin) (Transm)
AD 1516	Erasmus publishes a Greek-Latin parallel New Testament (Transm)
AD 1517	Luther starts the Protestant Reformation
AD 1526	Tyndale publishes the first English New Testament from Greek (Transl) (Transm)
AD 1539	The Great Bible published in English as the first authorized Bible of the Church of England (Transl)
AD 1551	Present system of verses added
AD 1611	King James Version published in English (Transl)
AD 1946–1956	981 Essene manuscripts found in Dead Sea caves (Old Testament) (Transm)
AD 1978	New International Version published in English (Transl)
AD 1989	New Revised Standard Version published in English (Transl)
AD 2011	Common English Bible Version published in English (Transl)

REVEAL (10-15 minutes)

SAY: Spend some time thinking about these questions and recording your answers in your journals. In a few minutes, I will call us back together to review and would love to hear some of your thoughts and answers then.

[After seven to eight minutes, call the group back together and ask the questions out loud, calling for a few volunteers to share their thoughts on each question.]

Journal Questions
1. How do you think differently about the Bible after today's lesson?
2. What is your personal understanding of inspiration?
3. What are some ways that you think other people understand inspiration, and how does that affect the way they treat the Bible?
4. Does God still speak to us through the Bible today? How?

BUILD (10-12 minutes)

The Translators Late Show

[Divide the group into four teams, and assign each team one of the four translator descriptions in the Student Journal: Jerome, John Wycliffe, King James, and The Essenes.]

SAY: It's amazing to think about how many people God has used over thousands of years to allow us to compile the Bible we have today. I've assigned each team an important person or group involved in the transmission and translation of the Bible. I want your team to determine how your translator would have answered the two questions listed in the Student Journal. Each team should select a representative to play the part of their translator in a "Late Show"–style interview format where they'll answer these questions.

[Give the teams three to five minutes to read and discuss. Then begin the interviews. Welcome the four guests as a talk-show host would, and have them sit at the front of the room. Be creative! Have fun with the talk-show format. If you have access to audio, play theme music as the guests are introduced and enter the room. Then ask each question to the four guests.]

ASK:
1. What inspired you to translate the Bible?
2. Tell us what's special about your Bible translation.

AFTER (5 minutes)

[Invite the students to participate in an After activity. Send them a reminder during the week.]

My Favorite Verse

SAY: Sometime this week, look up a favorite Bible verse on *www.biblegateway.com*. Select three different translations of the verse and note the differences and similarities. Finish by writing the verse in your own words.

An Encouraging Word

SAY: Sometime this week, find a Bible verse that would be an encouragement to a friend. Use *www.biblegateway.com* to choose the most appropriate translation. Text or direct-message this verse to your friend.

Inspiration Transmitted

SAY: Sometime this week, take a picture, or series of pictures, representing how you feel about God's faithfulness through the processes in the history of the Bible. Post it on social media with *#fathombible*. What image helps you to reflect on inspiration, transmission, and translation?

PRAYER

SAY: Let's all say this closing prayer out loud together.

God over all of time, we thank you for your great kindness and care in providing us with the Bible. Help us, in Jesus' name, to understand its life-changing message of love. Amen.

FATH●M
The Genres in the Bible

Summary

Students will gain an understanding of the different genres in the Bible and how these genres affect the interpretation of Scripture.

Overview

- **Sync** the differences among genres through a group activity that focuses on interpreting the same message in different ways.
- **Tour** through an overview of the seven genres of biblical literature.
- **Reveal** awareness of the different genres in the Bible by writing a poem or song in the style of one of the seven Bible genres.
- **Build** understanding about the importance of recognizing different genres in the Bible through an interactive mapping exercise.
- **After** the lesson, contextualize understanding of the seven genres in the Bible with activities throughout the week.

Anchor Point

- 2 Timothy 2:15—*Make an effort to present yourself to God as a tried-and-true worker, who doesn't need to be ashamed but is one who interprets the message of truth correctly.*

Supplies

- Student Journals
- Pens/pencils
- Two small baskets or bowls
- Index cards for "Movie Madness Matchup"
- Chalkboard or dry-erase board
- Students' smartphones

Parent E-mail

As we continue our study on how to read and understand the Bible, this week we will discuss the different literary genres in the Bible. We'll explore how to ask questions based on the type of literature we encounter when reading the Bible. Here are some ways to engage this week:

- Have your child show you the Bible Genre Guide they have been given (copies are in the Student Journal).
- Reorganize your DVD or book collection as a family, arranging them by genre. Use the Bible Genre Guide to consider how the Bible has different genres.

Leader Notes

The goal of this lesson is to introduce students to the different literary genres of the Bible. The hope is to give students a new confidence in reading their Bibles. Learning about the literary genres in the Bible helps students practice even more discernment in their reading of the Bible. In your study, you will find yourself naturally drawn to different types of genres. Focus your teaching in this lesson on the material where you are the most passionate so that this passion can be passed on to your students.

Theology and Commentary

What Genres Are in the Bible?

There are two questions we usually ask before we decide to watch a movie or read a book:

1. What kind of movie/book is it? (comedy, action, romance, horror, and so forth)
2. What's it about? (basic plot and story information)

Obtaining simple answers to these two questions typically convinces us whether we should watch a movie or read a book. These answers provide a framework for our experience. This lesson will deal primarily with the first question and how it affects the way we read different genres within the Bible. We are always encountering genres in all aspects of life. Each genre comes with its set of understood rules. When we don't pay attention to and follow those rules, we risk misunderstanding. This is true with literary genres of the Bible—the better we recognize and comprehend the rules of the genre, the greater our chance of understanding.

Stories

The stories of the Bible are primary stories about history. For context, they will often include historical reference points, such as genealogies, to educate the audience on the background of important characters. History in the ancient world was not understood the way we understand it now, as a precise, chronological progression through the story. Instead, the historical stories in the Bible are more interested in the narrative aspects of history and the meaning of the story. Other stories in the Bible are told as morality plays or parables. We should understand the Gospels as stories, but remember that they are unique in their focus on the person and work of Jesus. It is important for us to attempt to understand the main idea of the story—instead of getting too focused on details we choose to emphasize.

Law

The five books of the Torah/Pentateuch focus on God's formation of the people of Israel. These books primarily deal with the covenant God made with Israel through Moses. The books are linked together through the themes of obedience, worship, and rebellion. These writings should be understood in light of the covenants between God and Israel. Youth will understand comparisons to historical documents they have studied in school like the Constitution, the Bill of Rights, or the Magna Carta.

Wisdom

Wisdom literature focuses on "applying God's truth to your life so that your choices will indeed be godly."[1] Wisdom writings are poetic, observational, and comparative. They typically use simple verse patterns to compare and contrast axioms about the facts of life. While they are typically bound by poetic structure, Wisdom writings are more empirical than theoretical. These practical writings were often written by thought-leaders and philosophers. They were collected as life instructions to be passed down within families and communities to young people (father to son, teacher to pupil). Youth throughout history were often encouraged to learn and memorize Wisdom writings as part of their spiritual formation and development. We should be careful not to read universal truth, promises, or guarantees about life into Wisdom writings.

Psalms

The Psalms are the honest prayers and songs of God's people. While we know the historical context for some (Psalm 51 refers to David's sin with Bathsheba), they are universal in their appeal to our shared emotions and experiences. Readers should remember that the Psalms use figurative language to express emotional and spiritual realities. We don't read songs and poems the same way we do legal documents, letters, or stories.

The Prophets

The prophets spoke, wrote, and acted as the mouthpiece of God. They starkly rebuked Israel for its disobedience when God's people failed to hold up their side of the Mosaic covenant. The prophets used vivid and shocking imagery to illustrate Israel's rebellion and God's judgment. Social justice was a primary concern for the prophets as they emphasized Israel's failure to become the nation that God desired them to be. While the message of judgment is intense, these books also

1. Gordon D. Fee and Douglas Stuart, How to Read the Bible for All Its Worth: A Guide to Understanding the Bible (Grand Rapids, MI: Zondervan, 1981), 225.

speak of a hope for the future, ultimately fulfilled in Jesus. We should read the prophets with a clear understanding of both the Law (past) and the Gospels (future). Youth will understand the Prophets as an Act II-style genre—or the second movie in a trilogy that can even feel dark or unfinished (*The Empire Strikes Back, Lord of the Rings: The Two Towers, The Dark Knight*).

Letters

The New Testament consists largely of letters, sometimes called epistles. Early church leaders like Paul, Peter, and James wrote these letters to congregations across the Mediterranean world as the church expanded. While the letters address specific situations of doctrine, worship, and Christian living in those congregations, their messages are also deeply universal. The letters were read, copied, and passed around among the early churches, who were able to glean insights even though they were not the original audience. Today we continue to learn from these letters by following their example.

Apocalyptic Writings

Apocalyptic writings are the most unusual genre for modern audiences. They largely consist of divine revelations concerning major world events (for instance, the end times) where God intervenes directly in remarkable ways. They are a unique combination of many of the other genres— Letters, Prophets, and Stories. For example, Revelation uses both the cultural imagery of the first century and the prophetic imagery of the Old Testament to convey a message to the churches of the time. John uses coded numbers, symbols, and metaphors concerning political conflicts that his audience would understand (666 and the Beast as Nero Caesar). He also uses references from Daniel and other Old Testament Apocryphal writings (Babylon, the Dragon, and the Woman). The more we connect the images of the Apocalyptic books back to their original context, instead of our current world, the better our grasp of the intended message will be. While the imagery in these writings can sometimes be frightening, the central theme of these books is God's reign over evil in the world. Apocalyptic writings—whether understood literally or allegorically—convey the hope of God's victory to those struggling to find meaning within difficult life circumstances. Modern readers should be careful not to carelessly assign ancient apocalyptic symbols to modern headlines.

Leader Reflection

During a high school English class, I engaged the Bible seriously as literature for the first time. It felt almost sacrilegious to pose questions about the sacred text the same way I had *Grapes of Wrath* or *Hamlet*. I was afraid that studying the Bible this way would lessen its authority. Instead, I found joy in studying the Bible this way. Old stories and verses I thought I already understood came bursting back to life. Without an understanding of the different literary genres in the Bible, characters, scenes, dialogue, instructions, and settings become confusing and irrelevant. We desperately need to understand how to read and understand God's story, not just for knowledge and revelation, but also so we may understand the role we play in God's story as it unfolds today. As you prepare to teach, pray that God would give you a renewed desire to study and understand the Scriptures.

NOTES

SYNC (10-15 minutes)

High-Energy Option—Movie Madness Matchup

[Before the lesson, secure two baskets or bowls. Using the lists below, make Genre Cards and Line Cards. Place the Genre Cards in one basket and the Line Cards in the other. Place the baskets next to each other at the front of the room. Write out the five game genre options where everyone in the room can easily see them. Divide the group into two teams. Select which team will go first.]

SAY: We're going to play an acting game. I need a volunteer from the first team to choose one Genre Card and one Line Card. You are going to read the movie line that you selected in the style of the genre that you selected—as if you are auditioning for a role in that movie. You may say the line only once. Your team will get thirty seconds to guess the correct genre from the five possible choices. Teams get one guess per round. If they are correct, your team is awarded ten points. There are no steals.

[Play back and forth until you run out of cards (ten turns). Make sure the players don't put the cards back into the baskets during play.]

Genres for Movie Madness Matchup Genre Cards

[Make two cards for each genre.]

Comedy, Action, Horror, Western, Romance.

Movie Lines for Movie Madness Matchup Line Cards

[Make one card for each line.]

"You must be crazy coming in here like this."
"Did you call an ambulance yet?"
"Was that supposed to scare me?"
"I just can't leave you alone."
"He died a warrior's death."
"I'm moving to Florida."
"I miss our long walks in the park."
"He was like this when I got here."
"I would prefer that you not look at me like that."
"You have no proof of anything."

x

ASK:
1. What was the hardest genre to act out? What was the hardest to guess? Why?
2. How did the genres affect the meaning of the words? Would the words mean the same things in different contexts?

SAY: This activity was built on our understandings of genres. Today we will explore the different genres of writing in the books of the Bible.

Low-Energy Option—Remaking Pinocchio

[Divide the class into four groups and number them.]

SAY: Each group is going to work together to retell a very famous story. Group One will be telling the story as a comedy, Group Two as a tragedy, Group Three as an action/adventure story, and Group Four as a horror story.

[If you need more than four small groups, you can add a western version and/or a romance version.]

SAY: Each group will work together to rewrite the famous story of Pinocchio in their assigned genre. Be creative and make as many changes to the story as you need. You'll have eight minutes to write a synopsis of your Pinocchio remake. When finished, each group will present a short synopsis of their "new" Pinocchio story.

[Any famous story or fairy tale may be used for this section. Whatever story you choose, encourage your students to find a short synopsis of it online. Give the groups time to write the story and then present it to the rest of the class.]

ASK:
1. What stayed the same and what changed in everyone's Pinocchio retelling?
2. How did the genre affect the way you put together the story?
3. How did it change the way you read the story?

SAY: This activity was built on our understandings of genres. Today we will explore the different genres of writing in the books of the Bible.

TOUR (15-20 minutes)

ASK: "How would you classify and shelve the Bible in a library?"[2] If the Bible was a movie, what genre would it be?

SAY: We all understand how genres work. You all have a favorite type of movie or a favorite type of book. All stories have a genre. All stories in a given genre share similar characteristics, styles, and formats that guide you in how to understand the story. Today we are going to learn about the different genres within the Bible and how they help tell the deeper story of Scripture. As we go, remember that the Bible was written for us, but not to us. Each book of the Bible has an original audience in mind, and that influences the style in which it was written.

[Use the included Fathom Bible Genre Guide, included in the Student Journal and at the beginning of this Leader Guide, for your discussion.]

SAY: Learning how to read and think about the different genres in the Bible will help us ask the right questions of the text and come to a better understanding of its meaning. I'm going to divide you into seven groups *(Stories, Law, Wisdom, Psalms, The Prophets, Letters, Apocalyptic Writings)* and assign each group one of the seven genres we're going to study today. I'm going to give you five minutes to read about your genre in your Student Journals and put together a short skit explaining to the rest of the class how to read and understand the genre.

[Give the groups time to prepare and then present their skits.]

2. Scot McKnight, *The Blue Parakeet: Rethinking How You Read the Bible* (Grand Rapids, MI: Zondervan, 2008), 58.

Leader Guide • Lesson 2

REVEAL (10-15 minutes)

Write a Psalm

SAY: We've seen in today's lesson how the different styles of writing in the Bible require different types of questions for our understanding. The different genres also allow us to experience a variety of emotional and instructional content regarding the story of God and the world.

ASK: If you could write a short, simple song to God about how you are feeling about life right now, what would you write? Go to the My Psalm section of your Student Journals and take a few minutes to write a simple, honest poem or song chorus that expresses your emotions.

[Give the students six or seven minutes and then ask three or four volunteers to share their psalms aloud.]

BUILD (10-15 minutes)

SAY: Draw a quick, simple map to your house from the church in your Student Journal. Don't use street names or landmarks at all. It should take you one or two minutes.

ASK: Would your map make sense to someone who had never been to your house?

[Allow for discussion.]

SAY: Now draw a new, more detailed second map to your house including a few street names and at least five specific landmarks. I will give you four or five minutes.

ASK: How is this map different from your first map? Would it make more sense to someone seeing it for the first time?

SAY: Now pull up interactive directions to your house on your phones. What important steps were left out on your first and second map drawings?

SAY: The first map is not wrong—it simply represents a limited understanding. Often, we read the Bible backwards—expecting even metaphors and symbolic imagery to make sense in a literal context. We must remember that the Bible is written for us, but not to us. We are also quick to dismiss a verse or passage of Scripture if we feel we already understand it. Sometimes, learning more about a passage that we think we already understand can help us hear a fresh message from the Holy Spirit.

ASK: How can understanding different genres help us get a better understanding of what the Bible means today?

AFTER (5 minutes)

[Invite the students to participate in one of the After activities. Send them a reminder during the week.]

Bible Genre Selfies

SAY: Take some time this week to take seven selfies—each one with a different expression that you believe represents a genre in the Bible. Have fun with this! Group them together or post them separately on social media with #fathombiblegenres.

Bible Genre Prayer

SAY: Take some time every day this week to write a two- or three-sentence short prayer. Create each one in the style of a different Bible genre. Write each one on a note card and make them your daily prayers.

Our Epistle

SAY: Working with other friends, write a short letter to our church in the way early church leaders like Paul wrote to local churches. With a positive tone, address concerns and areas that you feel need new consideration or attention. Encourage the church by spotlighting the ways you feel like it is doing well. Volunteer specific help and leadership that you would be willing to provide in order to facilitate new ideas. Return the letter to your youth leader and ask that it be read to church leaders.

PRAYER

SAY: Let's all say this closing prayer out loud together.

God of all wisdom, we praise you for your creativity in how you have expressed your story through the different genres of the Bible. Help us, in Jesus' name, to think well as we encounter each book contained within it. Amen.

FATH●M
The Storylines of the Bible

Summary

Students will gain an understanding of the Bible's storylines and how they help us understand the story of God and creation.

Overview

- **Sync** the way we understand stories through a group activity.
- **Tour** through an overview of the central storylines in the Bible.
- **Reveal** the way these storylines continue in our lives and help us understand our faith.
- **Build** understanding about how the meaning of a story shapes the way we tell it.
- **After** the lesson, look for these biblical storylines in personal Bible study and every day in the world around us.

Anchor Point

- Deuteronomy 6:5-7—*Love the LORD your God with all your heart, all your being, and all your strength. These words that I am commanding you today must always be on your minds. Recite them to your children. Talk about them when you are sitting around your house and when you are out and about, when you are lying down and when you are getting up.*

Supplies

- Student Journals
- Pens or pencils
- Bell or other buzzer
- Index cards
- Basket or bowl
- Colored pencils or highlighters (multiple sets of red, blue, purple, yellow, orange, and green)

Parent E-mail

In this week's lesson, we'll learn about the six major storylines in the Bible: Create, Invite, Act, Redeem, Experience, and Hope. Students will be encouraged to see these storylines both in the Bible and in their lives today. Here are some ways to engage this week:

- Attempt to identify some of these storylines in a TV show that you watch as a family.
- Ask youth to explain the storylines in their own words during a family dinner.

Leader Notes

The purpose of this lesson is to introduce students to the storylines of the Bible. Make sure students understand that these storylines are about the larger story of God and creation. They are not limited to the writings of the Bible and are still at work in our lives today. These storylines are key characteristics of God's work. Identifying them will both help students understand the Scriptures better and bring the sacred words of the Bible to life.

Theology and Commentary

The Seven Basic Plots

There are two questions we usually ask or investigate before we decide to watch a movie or read a book:

- What kind of movie/book is it? (comedy, action, romance, horror, and so forth)
- What's it about? (basic plot and story information)

Our last lesson dealt with the biblical-studies equivalent of the first question—genres. This lesson will deal with the second question concerning the Bible: What's it about?

In 2004, Christopher Booker published the book *The Seven Basic Plots: Why We Tell Stories*. In it, he proposed that there are seven basic plots in all of the stories we know, write, read, and tell. The basic plots are: Overcoming the Monster, Rags to Riches, The Quest, Voyage and Return, Comedy, Tragedy, and Rebirth.[1] Every story is built around either one or a combination of these seven general plots. The most successful books, stories, musicals, plays, and TV shows typically employ many of the seven basic plots.

The Fathom Storylines of the Bible

We can see a version of Booker's basic plots in the story of the Bible. In this lesson, we will refer to these as the Fathom Bible Storylines. These storylines—**Create, Invite, Act, Redeem, Experience,** and **Hope**— are the major threads of the larger story found in the Bible about the relationship between God and creation. Teaching students to identify these storylines in a passage of Scripture will help them to tether the verses to the larger context.

The accompanying visual (included in the front of this book) shows the storylines designed to look like a chart for subway lines. This is a great way to explain how the storylines work in the Bible. Sometimes subway lines move together, side by side, and at other times lines veer

1. Christopher Booker, *The Seven Basic Plots: Why We Tell Stories* (New York, NY: Continuum, 2004).

drastically off on their own course. Ultimately, they are helping people move from one place to another in a very large and confusing city, much like the storylines found in the Bible help to move us through the story of God and God's people.

The Foundation of Exegesis

Much like a subway system, the Bible can be very confusing on first glance. It is an incredibly complex book written by dozens of authors over hundreds of years. These authors spoke different languages, lived in different cultures, told different stories, and wrote in entirely different ways. Remember, our strategy for reading the Bible reminds us that it was written for us, but not to us. How, then, can we understand what is being said about God and how it applies to us?

In the first three lessons of this study, we're focusing on the history of the Bible, the genres of biblical literature, and the storylines found within the biblical narrative. These key concepts form the foundation for a practice called *exegesis*. Exegesis is the process through which we analyze and interpret the Bible so that we can understand what the Bible was saying within its historical and cultural context. When we apply all of these concepts together, we can analyze Scripture and discover how what God did a thousand years ago still applies to our lives today.

Leader Reflection

On a summer youth mission trip several years ago, we had a free evening. Desiring for our students to experience immersion in the culture we were serving, I took them to a Shakespeare festival featuring a performance of *The Merchant of Venice*. Five minutes into the performance, I had no idea what was going on, and neither did the youth. I hadn't thought about what it would be like trying to absorb, digest, and understand the early Modern English of Shakespeare in a live setting. *"I have no idea what is happening,"* I could hear our youth whispering to one another. Twenty minutes into the play, I decided this had been a bad idea.

But something happened a few minutes later. Everything started to make sense. We could finally understand what was happening. Everyone started having a good time—fully captivated by the story being acted out. We were even laughing at the punchlines. Everyone got it. "How do you think we came to understand everything so well?" I asked later. One youth answered, "I think it's because we understand *story*. We read books and watch movies and tell stories—we are surrounded by stories. Once we got enough information to put together the plot, it was easier to follow—even through the twists and turns."

She was right. We *get* story. Maybe much of our confusion with the Bible has to do with the fact that we haven't taken the time to grasp its plots and storylines. This lesson is designed to help students learn those storylines so that they can better navigate the Scriptures. As you prepare, pray that God would help your group grasp the big story of God. Pray that the Spirit would bring clarity and enthusiasm to your teaching.

NOTES

SYNC (10-15 minutes)

High-Energy Option—Movie Words

[Write out the names of ten popular movies on index cards. Divide the group into two teams. Use a bell or other type of buzzer and place it on a table at the front of the room. Stand behind the table.]

SAY: We're going to play a game that will test your movie knowledge. I need one contestant from each team to come to the front of the room for the first face-off challenge.

SAY: I'm going to show the two contestants the name of a movie. The first player to hit the buzzer will state how many clue words she needs to help the rest of her team guess the movie correctly. If it will take more than one word, the other player can either challenge the first team to try it or offer to use fewer words to help the second team name the movie. This goes back and forth until one player challenges the other team to make the attempt.

SAY: Clue words cannot be names of characters, actors or actresses, or words that are part of the title. You may not make any motions or give any additional hints. You may use only the number of words agreed to during the face-off. If you break any of these rules, the other team will receive ten points. Teams have thirty seconds to correctly guess the movie from the clues given. Each team is allowed one guess. If they are correct, they receive ten points. If they are wrong, the other team receives ten points.

[Play back and forth, using new volunteers for each round, until you run out of movies.]

ASK:
1. Which were the easiest movies to guess? What did they have in common?
2. How important was the plot, or story, of a movie? Did it make it easier for you to create clues?
3. What makes a story memorable?

SAY: This activity was based on our understanding of stories and the way they stick out in our memory. Today we're going to explore the different storylines in the Bible and how they influence our faith.

Low-Energy Option—One Word at a Time[2]

SAY: I'm giving everyone a card and a pen. I want you to write one random word on the card. It could be a noun, an adjective, or the name of your pet cat. It doesn't matter. When you're finished, fold the card in half and place it in this basket.

[Give the students a moment to write down their words and place the cards in the basket.]

SAY: We are going to play a game where we make up stories—one word at a time. Place yourselves in small groups of six to eight. Each group should get in a circle. I need one person in each group to volunteer to start the story—with just one word. As you go around the circle, each person will add one word to the story. You can't use the same word twice. You have three minutes. Go!

[Give the students three minutes to create their stories.]

SAY: Great job, everyone! Now we're going to add a small wrinkle. I'm going to give three people in each group one of the random words from the basket. Don't let anyone see the word on your card. Play like before, except the students with assigned words must pass until they can use their word in a way that makes sense in their group's story. After a student uses an assigned word, she or he joins in the game as usual. The first group to use all three of their assigned words wins.

[Give the students three minutes to create their stories and use all three words.]

ASK:
1. What kinds of words were easier to fit into the stories—verbs, nouns, adjectives, adverbs?
2. Did the story progress as you thought it would after you added your word? How did your idea for the story change after someone else's word choice?
3. What makes a story memorable?

SAY: This activity was based on our understanding of stories and how we tell them. Today we're going to explore the different storylines in the Bible and how they influence our faith.

2. Based on the activity at *http://dramaresource.com/one-word-at-a-time/* (accessed December 2016).

TOUR (20 minutes)

ASK: What are your favorite stories? Why?

[Spend about a minute encouraging the students to talk about their favorite stories.]

SAY: Today we are going to learn about the different storylines that work together to make up the big story of Scripture. Turn to the Fathom Bible Storylines chart at the front of your Student Journals. Here you'll see a list of all distinct storylines found throughout the Bible.

[Show the students a map of the New York City MTA Subway line (http://web.mta.info/maps/submap.html) alongside the Bible Storylines chart in their Student Journals.]

ASK: Has anyone ever ridden on a subway? What was it like to navigate a subway system? How could the storylines in the Bible work like a subway system?

[Affirm every response.]

SAY: The Fathom Bible Storylines chart is designed to look like a chart of the New York City Subway for a reason. You'll see on the subway map that sometimes the lines cover the same ground, and other times the subway lines veer off on their own course. The storylines in the Bible work the same way. Sometimes two or three different storylines run through the same story.

SAY: Let's learn the six storylines in the Bible and the questions we should ask when we identify these storylines at work. These elements are always at work in God's story. I'll need six volunteers to read through the different storylines.

[Assign one student to read out the explanation for each of the storylines.]

The Fathom Storylines of the Bible

Create

God is always creating and re-creating. We see this when God acts in the world in new and surprising ways. The question we should ask about these passages is: *What new thing is God doing?*

Invite

God is constantly inviting humanity into a full and meaningful life, and a divine relationship. This is seen in the covenants that God makes with humanity throughout history. The question we should ask about these passages is: *What is God's invitation?*

Act

When God offers an invitation to humanity, God also gives humanity a choice in how they respond. We can see this in the way biblical figures decide to obey and accept or disobey and reject God's invitation. Many of the Bible's stories are about how individuals respond to God's reign and rule. The question we should ask about these passages is: *How is this person or group choosing to respond to God's invitation?*

Redeem

God's work is about the redemption of all things. We see this redemption most clearly in the life and work of Jesus. Followers of Jesus are redeemed and join with the Holy Spirit to become agents of God's restorative work in the world. The question we should ask about these passages is: *How is God working through this person, group, or situation to redeem, restore, and rebuild?*

Experience

God gives wisdom and direction for how to live a life empowered by the Holy Spirit. We see this in the writings of leaders who have left us a legacy of instruction from their encounters with God. This is where authentic faith meets real life in the quest for truth. The question we should ask about these passages is: *How is the Holy Spirit leading and directing in these situations?*

Hope

God provides hope for the future. We see this often in prophetic writings by oppressed people in desperate situations. In the midst of what seem like impossible circumstances, God assures us of God's reign. Though things may not be right in the present, God promises a different outcome for those who endure. The question we should ask about these passages is: *How is God assuring those in despair that they can have great faith in hope to come?*

Navigating the Storylines

SAY: Divide up into groups of three to five. You're going to work together to identify the genre and storylines for each Scripture passage listed. Use the Fathom Bible Genre Guide and Fathom Bible Storylines chart from your Student Journal. You may find multiple storylines in each story—just like when the subway lines run together. Use colored pencils or highlighters to highlight sentences or phrases that reflect each separate storyline.

[Give the students ten minutes to work, then review answers together.]

Genesis 4:9-16
Psalm 13
Jeremiah 31:31-34
John 3:1-8
Romans 5:6-11
Revelation 16:1-7

REVEAL (10 minutes)

SAY: The Fathom Storylines we've learned to recognize in the Bible help us understand the continuing story of God's relationship with the church and the world. Spend a few minutes quietly reflecting on the following questions:

1. How does understanding these storylines help you understand God's relationship with creation?
2. How do you see these storylines playing out in your own faith?
3. Which storyline connects with you most strongly? Why?

[After five or six minutes, allow the students a chance to volunteer some of their answers to the whole group. If your group is quiet, start things moving by sharing one of your own answers.]

BUILD (10-15 minutes)

New Story, Same As the Old?

SAY: Choose one of the Bible passages that you looked at in our prior activity. Rewrite the passage using modern-day language. If it's a psalm, you could make it a song. If it's a story, you could give it a modern setting. I'll give you five or six minutes to think and write.

[Allow the students time to write, then invite several students to share their new versions.]

ASK:
1. How did rewriting the story in a new context change the storyline of the passage?
2. Did rewriting the story give you any new insights on the meaning of the passage?
3. How important is it to identify the storylines involved when reading the Bible?

AFTER (5 minutes)

[Invite the students to participate in one of these After activities. Send them a reminder during the week.]

I Walk the Storyline

SAY: During your personal Bible study time this week, make notes of where you see the six storylines in the Bible: create, invite, act, redeem, experience, and hope. While reading and reflecting on the verses, ask yourself which of the storylines you see at work. Keep these notes and reminders in the margin of your Bible or a journal. If you are reading through a chapter or book of the Bible, track the progression and overlap of the storylines. Use colored pencils or highlighters to mark storylines.

#FathomStoryline

SAY: The great thing about the storylines we see in the Bible is that they are still playing out as part of God's story today. Take some pictures this week of things in your world in which you see the six storylines of the Bible at work: create, invite, act, redeem, experience, and hope. Post the pictures on social media with *#fathomstoryline*, and comment on which storyline you see.

Living Out the Lines

SAY: Spend some time this week reflecting on how God has worked in your life's story. Journal about how you see God actively writing an incredible saga through your journey. Identify and explore all six storylines in the past and present. Ask a friend to do the same, and share your reflections with each other.

PRAYER

SAY: Let's all say this closing prayer out loud together.

God of every moment, we glorify you for your care as you have crafted every moment of history to tell us your story. Help us, in Jesus' name, to truly fathom the constructs of that story—and to find our own storylines within them—as we study the Bible. Amen.

FATH●M
How to Interpret the Bible

Summary

Students will learn and practice how to read and study the Bible using the Fathom Exegetical Process.

Overview

- **Sync** the importance of the concepts of light and context when reading the Bible.
- **Tour** through the Fathom Exegetical Process.
- **Reveal** how the Bible can be applied to our lives using *Lectio Divina* as part of the Fathom Exegetical Process.
- **Build** confidence in using the Fathom Exegetical Process by using the process on a favorite hymn or praise song.
- **After** the lesson, encourage students to practice using the Fathom Exegetical Process at home.

Anchor Point

- Psalm 119:105—*Your word is a lamp before my feet and a light for my journey.*

Supplies

- Student Journals
- Pens or pencils
- One flashlight for every fourteen students
- Study Bibles, commentaries (for Acts and 1 John), Bible atlases, concordances, and/or digital copies of these from online sites such as www.ministrymatters.com
- One student's smartphone
- Candles (optional)

Parent E-mail

This week we will be completing our study on how to read and understand the Bible. We will be learning about a method to help interpret the Bible and apply it to everyday life. This exegetical method is built around light as a metaphor for how we can go about studying the Bible. Here are some great ways to engage this week:

- Ask your youth to lead a short family Bible study using what they have learned these last four weeks.
- Make a gift of a new journal to encourage their continued study of the Bible.

Leader Notes

The psalmist declares in Psalm 119:105, "Your word is a lamp before my feet and a light for my journey." We will use light as a metaphor to learn how to interpret the Bible. This process will move the reader from observation to personal application through an inductive study. We strive to faithfully understand the Scriptures and better hear God's voice.

Theology and Commentary

The Exegetical Process

Dr. Roy Heller, Associate Professor of Old Testament at Perkins School of Theology at Southern Methodist University, has stated that "most people view the Bible as either an answer-book, a textbook, or a workbook."[1] When people treat the Bible as an answer-book, they expect it to respond to their questions. It's only useful until it cannot provide an answer to a question it never asked. Others treat the Bible as a textbook, an educational and historical guide to what God has done in the past. It's good information to know, but not dynamic and relevant.

We should view the Bible as a workbook. We should allow ourselves time to work through the text as it is presented first, only afterward adding in our current situations to work out an answer that meets our needs while being faithful to the original contexts. This lesson will teach students the key elements of an exegetical method that allows us to use the Bible as a workbook in our lives.

A good inductive exegetical method is sequential. It follows a logical, intuitive pattern. While the steps are designed to be interdependent, concluding with application, God can certainly speak to us at any juncture in the process. The discipline of an exegetical approach helps develop faithfulness and diligent study, but at the same time, it is merely a tool. An exegetical method should start with setting a passage within its larger context followed by an examination of the passage. This work begins with identifying the proper literary genre. The questions provided for specific genres and storylines in our previous lessons would be helpful in these steps. The next step in the process involves a more precise analysis and examination of the passage. Different translations, interpretations, perspectives, critiques, and assumptions about the passage should be consulted. This work is crucial to our final step—personal application. All of our prior work is brought to fruition in our application. The Spirit is at work throughout the process. The entire process should be presented as a holistic, comprehensive model.

1. Roy L. Heller, lecture, Perkins School of Youth Ministry, Dallas, TX, January 2014.

The Fathom Exegetical Process

Floodlight—The Big Picture
Flashlight—The Focused Context
Headlight—In Front of Us
Shadow—A Glimpse of Jesus
Laser—Personal Application

Leader Reflection

The discipline of exegetical Bible study helps to remind us of just how *real* the Scriptures are. These are more than characters on a page and stories for children—they are the witness of God's great story throughout our history. As you prepare, pray that God would give you the wisdom needed to grasp the material. Pray that God would give your students a deep hunger for the Bible.

NOTES

SYNC (10-15 minutes)

High-Energy Option—Flashlight Freeze

[This is an active, play-in-the-dark game. You will need a dimly lit area at minimum. Find a space that is good for running and hiding. Set up the boundaries of the game before you play. Take a flashlight (one for every fourteen students) apart into at least three pieces—the lens, the barrel, and the battery—and hide the pieces throughout the play area.]

SAY: I need one volunteer to be "IT." *[If you have more than fourteen players and are using two flashlights, have two ITS.]* Your goal is to tag the other players, which renders them inactive like freeze tag. There is no base. If the frozen player is tagged by another player, the frozen player can become active in the game again. The players' objective is to find the flashlight and assemble it. Once you put the flashlight together and get it working, you must find and shine the light on whoever is IT to end the game.

[Play as many times as you want in the time you have allotted for an activity. Use the questions below to complete the activity.]

ASK:
1. What was the most difficult part of the game?
2. How did you feel once the flashlight was found and assembled?
3. The Bible has been referred to as light or illumination. How do you think the Bible functions like a flashlight in the dark?

SAY: This game used light as an important element. Today we will learn a new way to study the Bible that uses different light sources as metaphors.

Low-Energy Option—Loopy Locution

SAY: Divide into four to six small groups. Work together to fill out the two "Loopy Locution" Words pages in your Student Journal. Don't look at the passage on the following two pages yet. After you are finished filling in all of the words, then turn the page and fill them into the passage provided there.

[If you have time, allow a representative from each group to share their funniest lines. Use the questions below to complete the activity.]

ASK:
1. Psalm 23 is a very familiar text. Even with the new words added in, did it still feel familiar? Why do you think that is?
2. How important is context to the things we read?
3. How important is context when reading the Bible?

SAY: This game used different words for a very famous passage of Scripture. Today we will learn a new way to study the Bible that will help us understand better how it can speak to us.

TOUR (15-20 minutes)

SAY: I need a volunteer to read Psalm 119:105 aloud. What do you think this verse is saying?

[Affirm all answers and invite thoughts from quieter students.]

SAY: Remember our strategy for reading the Bible: that it is written for us, but not to us. For us to best apply the Bible to our lives, we must first try to understand what it meant to its original audience. This process is called *exegesis*. I am going to teach you a process to use when studying your Bible to help you understand and apply what Scripture is saying. Like the verse we read from Psalms, this process plays with the metaphor that the Bible is a light for our journey and uses different sources of light as the steps of the process. These steps are floodlight, flashlight, headlight, shadow, and laser.

The Fathom Exegetical Process

Floodlight

ASK: What does a floodlight do? How is it used?

SAY: In the floodlight step, we identify the big picture in the passage we're analyzing. Floodlights illuminate large areas with wide, dispersed lighting. In this step, we connect the verse or passage to its place in the whole of the biblical narrative.

SAY: Some important questions to ask in this step are:

Where does this passage fall in the big story of the Bible? Which storyline is it emphasizing?

Flashlight

ASK: What kind of light does a flashlight produce? How is it used?

SAY: The flashlight stage focuses on the immediate context of the passage being studied. Flashlights illuminate smaller areas with directed, focused lighting. In this stage, we connect the verse or passage to its immediate surroundings.

SAY: Some insightful questions to ask in this step are:

What is the genre of the passage? Who was the original intended audience? What was its purpose to the original audience? What did it mean to them?

Headlight

ASK: What purpose does a headlight serve on a car?

SAY: In the headlight stage, we'll focus on what this passage is telling us about our present situation. Car headlights illuminate the road ahead of a moving vehicle with reflected, projected lighting. A headlight shows a progressing, dynamic pathway. We'll connect the verse or passage to our own day.

SAY: Some helpful questions to ask in this step are:

What could the passage be saying about God or God's reign today? What does this mean now to the church on the other side of the cross? How does this speak right now?

Shadow

ASK: What is a shadow?

SAY: We're going to use the idea of a shadow to illustrate a special step in our process—what the passage teaches us about Jesus. A shadow is produced when an object comes between a surface and a source of light. A shadow does not reflect or show light, but is evidence of the light. In this step, we connect the verses to the person and work of Jesus. The text might not speak about Jesus at all, but we can still learn something about his character, ministry, and context—even if it's simply humanity's great need for the redemption he provides.

SAY: A good question to ask in this step is:

How does this passage help me understand the person and work of Jesus?

SAY: Some useful tools to help you work through these first four steps are study Bibles, commentaries, Bible atlases, and concordances.

Laser

ASK: What is a laser? How are lasers used?

SAY: We're going to use a laser as the image for our final step in this process—personal application. Lasers illuminate tiny areas with powerful, focused light. Laser light is strong enough to cut through material objects and surfaces. In the laser stage, we connect the passage with a personal application specific to us. By this stage, you have gathered good information to help you understand the passage, and it is time to apply it. *Lectio Divina* (divine reading) can be a helpful practice before arriving at a personal application. In *Lectio Divina*, the reader simply reads or hears the passage with a clear mind, meditates in silence, and prays—listening for God's voice. Pay close attention to the words or phrases that stand out from your Bible reading. This pattern can be repeated multiple times. Don't rush to an answer in *Lectio Divina*, just listen.

SAY: Some reflective questions to ask in this step are:

What does the passage mean for me? How then shall I live?

Navigating the Method

SAY: Let's use the Fathom Exegetical Process together as a group.

[Use either 1 John 1:5-7 (medium length) or Acts 1:8 (shorter), depending on group size and time. Allow the students to use commentaries, study Bibles, Bible atlases, and concordances. If your group is larger than twelve, break up into two or three smaller groups for them to work together in. Guide the students through the work by giving them time between questions. As you go, record common, generalized answers for each category on dry-erase board, chalkboard, or personal notes. You may want these for the Reveal exercise later.]

Floodlight

SAY: Let's identify the floodlight—the big picture. Spend some time working together on this step in the process. Use the questions in your Student Journal to help you.

ASK: Where does it fall in the big story of the Bible?

ASK: Which storyline is it emphasizing?

Flashlight

SAY: Now let's identify the flashlight—the focused context. I'm going to give you a few minutes to work together on this step. Use the questions in your Student Guide to help you.

ASK: Who was the original intended audience?

ASK: What was the original purpose of the passage?

ASK: What is its genre?

Headlight

SAY: What could this passage be saying about God or God's reign today? *(rhetorical)* How does this speak right now? *(rhetorical)* Let's spend some time identifying the headlight—what this passage shows in front of us. Use the questions in your Student Journal to help you.

ASK: What are the differences between the original context and audience and today's context and audience?

ASK: What does this passage mean today?

Shadow

SAY: Let's look for the shadow in this passage. What can we learn about the person and work of Jesus here? Use the questions in your Student Journal to help you.

ASK: How does this passage help us understand the person and work of Jesus?

REVEAL (10 minutes)

Navigating the Method

SAY: Now that we have worked through the first four steps in our process, we are going to practice the fifth and final step—the laser, or personal application—using *Lectio Divina*. Spread out in the room with your Bibles and Student Journals. Find a space where you'll be able to avoid distractions while we focus. I'm going to light some candles around the room while you find your space for meditation. These candles will represent God's light and the illumination of the Scriptures.

SAY: We're going to start by clearing our minds with a few minutes of silence. Focus on your breathing.

SAY: I'm going to say, "Lord, speak. Your servant is listening" (1 Samuel 3:10) three times in thirty- to forty-second intervals over the next two minutes. You may join me in saying this aloud when I speak, or you can say it silently to yourself. Spend this time focused on listening to God.

[Repeat, "Lord, speak. Your servant is listening," three times, once every thirty to forty seconds.]

SAY: I'm going to slowly read aloud one verse from the passage that we worked through earlier. Pay attention to the word or words that stand out to you as I read. Record these words in your Student Journal.

[For 1 John 1, use verse 5; for Acts 1:8, use the entire verse. Read the verse three times aloud over the next three to four minutes.]

SAY: I'm going to give you two or three minutes to pray in silence as you continue to listen, asking God, *What does the passage mean for me today? How then shall I live?* As you review your notes from our earlier study and pray, use your Student Journal to write down your personal application.

[Close with this short prayer.]

SAY: Help us to hear your words, O God, and give us the courage to act upon them. Amen.

BUILD (10-15 minutes)

Shine a Light

SAY: We're going to practice the Fathom Exegetical Process on one of your favorite hymns/praise songs. It won't be quite the same as studying the Bible, but it will help us understand how to use the method. What is one of your favorite hymns or praise songs that we could study?

[Take suggestions from students. After several appropriate options have been suggested, have the students make a final decision on a song most of them know fairly well. Ask a volunteer to look up the lyrics on her or his phone and read them to the class.]

SAY: Divide into groups of three or four and use your Student Journal to walk through the Fathom Exegetical Process with this song.

[Give the students time to work through the Fathom Exegetical Process together.]

ASK:
1. What did you learn about this song?
2. How do you feel this method will help you learn new things from the Bible?

AFTER (5 minutes)

[You may select one or two of the following After activities for your group. Send them a reminder during the week.]

Rays-of-Light Photo Challenge

SAY: Capture an interesting picture of each example of light from the Fathom Exegetical Process (floodlight, flashlight, headlight, shadow, laser). Be as creative as you want! Post them to social media using *#fathombiblelights*, with comments about how you are seeing God's story in new ways through personal Bible study.

Using the Fathom Exegetical Process

SAY: Select a Bible passage from the list below and use the Fathom Exegetical Process to arrive at your personal application this week. Commit to sharing the highlights of your study with a small-group leader, youth leader, pastor, parent, or friend.

Jeremiah 29:8-14
Acts 8:26-40
Philippians 4:10-14

Choose to Act

SAY: With other friends from your group, find a way to serve in your local community this week. Allow this to be a response to God's invitation. Ask your youth leader to help you find some different opportunities to serve—food pantries, roadside cleanups, nursing homes, hospitals, homeless missions, military/veteran support, and so forth.

PRAYER

SAY: Let's all say this closing prayer out loud together.

God of wisdom, we humbly accept the gift you have given us in the Bible. Help us, in Jesus' name, to delight in its words as we find strength, hope, wisdom, and help in our lifelong study of them. Amen.

Explore More

How Jesus Used the Old Testament

Anchor Point
• Matthew 5:17-20

Summary

Consider how Jesus uses the Bible in different contexts and situations. Help youth understand how Jesus' knowledge of the Scriptures provided him with practical counsel in various situations.

Takeaways

• Jesus uses the Scriptures for personal devotion and encouragement.
• Jesus balances knowledge of the Scriptures with how they shape our action in real life—our devotion, integrity, and social holiness.

How the Books of the Bible Are Arranged

Anchor Point
• Deuteronomy 6:20-25

Summary

The Bible isn't arranged in chronological order or in the order in which they were written. Instead, the books of the Bible are arranged in a way that helps us understand the overarching narrative of God's relationship with humanity.

Takeaways

• The arrangement of the books in the Bible helps point us back to the big story.
• We should read the Bible with consideration for the way it's organized.

FATH●M

A deeper dive into understanding the key themes and storylines of the Bible.

Continue Your Journey Into God's Story With The Following Fathom Titles

The Bible
Where it came from and how to read it

The Beginnings
Genesis

The Passion
The Death and Resurrection of Jesus

The Wilderness
Exodus-Deuteronomy

The Coming of Jesus
The Birth of a Savior

The Birth of the Church
Acts 1-8

The Teachings of Jesus
Matthew-John

The Promised Land
Joshua-Judges

The Life in the Church 1
Romans-Philemon

The Life in the Church 2
Hebrews-Jude

The Birth of the Kingdom
From Saul to Solomon

The Wisdom of the Kingdom
Job – Song of Songs

The Spread of the Church
Acts 9-28

The Broken Kingdom
The Fall of Israel

The Leaders of the Church
Profiles in the New Testament

The Exile and Return
Ezra-Esther and the Minor Prophets

The Promise of the Future
Stories of Hope in Ruth, Isaiah & Micah

The Return of Jesus
Revelation

To learn more about all 18 Studies go to YouthMinistryPartners.com/Studies/Fathom

CPSIA information can be obtained
at www.ICGtesting.com
Printed in the USA
LVOW03s2222160517
534632LV00004B/11/P